ERASED
BUT NOT
FORGOTTEN

CONQUERING THE MISSION THEY NEVER PREPARED US FOR:
A VETERAN DAD'S GUIDE TO HEALING, FATHERHOOD,
AND FIGHTING FOR WHAT MATTERS MOST

PHIL CALCESE

Published by Made to Change the World™ Publishing
Nashville, Tennessee

ISBN: 978-1-956837-63-6 (print)
ISBN: 978-1-956837-64-3 (ebook)

Printed globally.

DEDICATION

To every father who has ever felt silenced, erased, or labeled as "unfit" because of the invisible wounds you carry—
This book is for you.

To the veterans who traded pieces of themselves for the freedom of others, only to return home
and fight a battle no one warned them about—
A battle not on foreign soil, but in courtrooms,
in quiet rooms, in broken systems,
and in the aching space between you and your children.

To the men who have fallen, the ones still standing,
and the ones who feel like giving up—
I see you. I honor you. I fight alongside you.

For every father who was told to "move on"
when all he wanted was to be present.
For the ones navigating silence, shame, and separation—
and still waking up with hope.
You are not weak for feeling this.
You are not broken because you care.
You are not invisible, even when the world tries to make you feel that way.

You are a warrior in the purest sense.
A father not defined by absence,
but by love that refuses to quit.

This book is a reminder:
You are not alone.
You are not forgotten.
And this journey? It's ours now.

TABLE OF CONTENTS

"I may be kept from your world,
but nothing can keep me from loving you.
My hands are still reaching."

ACKNOWLEDGMENTS

To my children:

There is no distance, no time, and no circumstance that could ever weaken the love I have for you. You are the very breath in my lungs and the fire in my soul. You are the reason I've kept going.

Though life has tried to build walls between us, I need you to know—those walls are powerless against a father's love. I have never stopped fighting for you, and I never will.

I am with you now.
I'll be with you tomorrow.
I'll be with you always—
In every sunrise, in every quiet moment, in every beat of your heart where you wonder if I still care… *I do*. I always have. I always will.

If you ever doubt, just close your eyes…
I'll meet you there, in whatever way you need me most.

I love you to the moon and back,
and I am here…
Always.

To my wife—Monica, your unconditional love, your fierce loyalty, and your belief in this mission have carried me through my darkest nights. You are my safe place, my partner, my heart. I love you more than words will ever be big enough to contain.

To my father—Dad, thank you for never giving up on us. You may have waited in silence, but you never disappeared. I couldn't understand the battle you fought for so many years until I found myself in the same one. Now I see it. You've given me hope that one day my children will recognize the same truth that took me more than thirty years to realize.

To my brothers and sisters who have walked this painful path with me—your courage, your vulnerability, and your determination to heal have inspired every page of this work.

To my Montgomery chosen family—you know who you are. You stepped in without hesitation, loved me without condition, and never once turned your back when the weight got heavy. You reminded me what home feels like, and what true connection looks like. I'm forever grateful to stand shoulder to shoulder with you.

To the Divine Kings container—led by Jerremy Newsome and Chuck Hogan, and held up by the strength of every man within it. Your unwavering loyalty, fierce brotherhood, and sacred space of truth gave me the strength to keep walking through the fire. In the moments when I felt most lost, you stood tall beside me. You reminded me that kings don't suffer in silence—we rise together.

To all the unshakable people in my life who showed up when others walked away—thank you. Your presence was oxygen when I was gasping for air.

To my mentors and coaches—Jon and Becca, you started as my running coaches, but you became so much more than that. You didn't just train my body—you helped me rebuild my spirit. Every push, every honest word, every mile we logged together reminded me that I still had something worth fighting for. You saw strength in me when I felt broken. You believed in my story before I had the courage to speak it. Thank you for helping me keep moving—on the trail, and in life.

To every brother-in-arms and every veteran dad still in the fight—you've given me the fire to keep going. This book is born from the same grit, loyalty, and love that you've shown me time and time again.

FOREWORD

I've seen combat. I've built runways in war zones and shelters after tsunamis. I've led men through chaos in ways most people will never understand. But nothing—absolutely nothing—was as exhausting or emotionally brutal as trying to hold my family together when my marriage unraveled.

Though she is no longer with us, my wife didn't keep the kids. But that didn't stop her from dragging me through years of emotional warfare, chaos, and instability. It was never about the truth. It was about control. Reputation. Payback. And in the middle of that storm, I was just trying to be a father.

That's why I said yes immediately when Phil asked me to write this foreword.

Because this book isn't just his story—it's mine too. It's every man's story who has felt the sting of being dismissed, distorted, or demonized for trying to show up for his kids. *Erased But Not Forgotten* pulls no punches. It's a raw, real, battle-tested account of what it's like to fight for your children in a world that doesn't always care if you're a good man—it just wants to know if you're the right narrative.

Phil doesn't just tell the truth. He reclaims it.
He turns pain into purpose.
And most importantly, he gives other fathers the one thing
we all needed but rarely got—hope.

If you're reading this and you're in the thick of it, I want you to
hear this from a man who made it through:

You're not weak.
You're not alone.
And you're not done.

You're a builder. A father. A fighter.
Keep going.

To Aidan and Gigi, Papa always loves you.

Chris Cronin
Retired Navy Seabee
Vice President, Clark Construction

Even from a distance,
love leaves a mark.

CHICAGO BUILT ME

Ever hear that saying, *"It's not where you start;*
it's where you finish"?

Sounds like a motivational quote on a t-shirt.
But let me tell you something that's a little more honest:
Where you start leaves a mark.

Chicago left plenty of them on me.

I grew up in the south suburbs—Woodridge, Bolingbrook,
Romeoville. I could probably still drive those streets in my
sleep. My childhood was like a game of musical chairs.
New apartment. New school. New friends. New rules.
Over and over again.

I used to think it was normal.
Honestly, I didn't know any different.

My parents split when I was around seven.
One day I had a dad. The next day, he was gone.

I don't remember much about that season.
What I do remember is what I was told:
"Your dad doesn't want anything to do with you."

You tell a little boy that enough times, he starts to believe it.
And I did.

My mom did what she could. She worked hard. She kept a
roof over our heads. She made sure there was food on the
table, even if it was sloppy joes or hamburger helper.
I never went hungry. But emotionally?
I was starving.

My mom remarried not long after the divorce.
I won't get into the details—out of respect for everyone
involved—but let's just say that relationship didn't give me
the model of manhood I needed.
He was barely older than me, and the dynamic felt more like
competition than parenting.

So I learned to adapt.
Learned to stay out of the house as much as possible.
I learned that sometimes it felt safer to be with friends or on
the street, than it did to sit at my own dinner table.

By the time I was in middle school,
I had become a master at fitting in.
New school? No problem.
New crowd? I could read the room in seconds.

New environment?
I'd blend in before the bell rang for first period.

That became my survival skill—
being whatever people needed me to be to stay accepted.

I wasn't the smartest kid in the room.
I wasn't the fastest.
But I was big.

By sixth grade, I was pushing 185 pounds. By seventh, I was
wrestling what felt like grown men. I always showed up on
the football field and there was zero quit in me. That bought
me some status. Coaches loved having me on the team. It felt
good to belong somewhere, even if it was just for a season.

But belonging isn't the same as *becoming*.

You can be part of something and still feel empty inside.
And that's exactly where I was.

I started chasing connection in all the wrong places—girls,
parties, weed, anything to feel something other than the ache
of not knowing who I really was. I couldn't sit with myself for
too long. It felt like there was too much noise in my head.
Too much I didn't want to face.

By the time I hit high school, things only got messier.
We moved again, this time to a nicer suburb called Palatine.
Complete culture shock.

I went from a lower-income, mixed neighborhood to a predominantly white, upper-class school. I showed up looking, talking, and acting completely different than everyone else.

I wore baggy clothes. I spoke with a different tone. I carried myself like someone from the other side of town.

And you know what happened?
I became the *"cool new kid."*
Not because I fit in, but because I didn't.

I remember kids telling me how much allowance they got every week—more than my mom made working overtime. I remember seeing parents buy their kids cars when they turned sixteen. Meanwhile, I was hustling side jobs just to be able to pay for all the responsibilities a young man has.

Sports kept me sane.
Football. Wrestling. Swimming.
Even water polo, believe it or not.
It gave me something to focus on,
somewhere to put my energy.

But after practice, I didn't go home.
I'd crash at a friend's house. In the apartment unit above us, older kids hung out. They didn't care where I came from—just whether I could hold my own.

I was chasing something I couldn't name—
belonging, connection, peace... maybe all of it.

I knew how to be liked.
I knew how to perform.
But I had no clue who *Phil* really was.

And the more I chased belonging, the more I drifted from anything that felt real.

Drinking started showing up more. Weed turned into other things—stuff I told myself was just "for fun" but really, it was escape. Not because I wanted to be *that guy,* but because it gave me a break from myself. For a few hours, I didn't have to feel the weight of not knowing my dad, the ache of being the outsider, or the shame of never feeling good enough.

And still—**nobody noticed.**
Or maybe they did.
But when you're good at keeping up appearances,
people stop asking questions.

The turning point came in the form of a random hallway conversation. I was walking to football practice, wearing my jersey, when an Army recruiter stopped me.

More on the details of that story soon enough!

Looking back now, I didn't just enlist in the Army that day.
I signed up for the next chapter of my life—
a chapter I thought would bring peace, purpose, and clarity.

What I didn't realize was that I was stepping into a system that would both build me up and try to break me down.

A system that would give me an identity…
and later, try to take it from me.

But that part of the story comes later.

For now, all I knew was this:

Chicago built me.
But the Army was about to change me.

SOUL WORK

INTRODUCTION
CHICAGO BUILT ME

You are not what you survived.
You are what you decided to build from it.

EXCERPT FROM THE BOOK:
"I knew how to be liked. I knew how to perform. But I had no clue who Phil really was."

REFLECTION PROMPTS:

1. What parts of your upbringing felt like survival, not childhood?

2. How did you learn to adapt—and what did it cost you?

3. When did you first start to feel like you were performing instead of *being*?

ACTION STEP:
Write down three survival skills you picked up as a kid.
Then ask yourself: *Do these still serve me, or are they holding me back now?*

MANTRA OF THE WEEK:
"I'm not who the world told me to be—
I'm who I chose to become."

Chapter 1

CAUGHT IN THE SYSTEM

When I think back on it, it feels like life moved fast after I signed those papers with the recruiter.

One minute, I was drifting through high school halls,
trying to keep my head above water.
The next, I was on a bus headed to basic training,
carrying nothing but a duffel bag and the hope that this
might finally give me the identity I'd been chasing.

And for a while, it did.

The Army gave me structure.
It gave me purpose.
It gave me a team.
I finally felt like I belonged to something bigger than myself.
I was no longer the kid trying to fit in—

I was part of something that demanded the best out of me, whether I felt like giving it or not.

I thrived under the structure.
I got promoted.
I built a reputation as someone you could count on.
I got good at saying "yes" to every opportunity,
every challenge, every mission.

And like a lot of young men in the military,
I eventually met someone I wanted to build a life with.
We were young. We had big dreams.
We believed in the idea of "forever."

Looking back, I know now how unprepared I was—
not just for marriage, but for real life beyond the mission.
I brought all my unhealed wounds into that relationship—
the abandonment, the performance mentality,
the silent pressure to always be "strong" and "in control."

She had her own story, her own wounds,
her own perspective.

I won't speak for her here. Out of respect for everyone involved, I'll simply say this: we were both doing the best we could with the tools we had at the time.

But marriage under military pressure is no small thing.
Deployments.
Training cycles.
Late nights.
Missed birthdays.

Hard conversations over patchy phone calls.
The kind of distance you can't measure in miles.

We tried.
God knows, we tried.

But the cracks started to show.

And when the marriage ended, I thought the hardest part
was walking away from the relationship.

I had no idea the real battle was just beginning.
And I truly had no idea that fatherhood itself was about to be
put on trial.

Maybe you've been there too.
Maybe you thought being a good dad would be enough.
Maybe you believed that love, effort, and presence would
carry weight in a courtroom.
Maybe you assumed that your service—your sacrifice—
would earn you some grace.

If any of that sounds familiar,
I want you to know something right now:
You are not crazy.
You are not alone.
And you are not the problem.

At first, I believed the court would see the truth—
that I was a good dad, that I loved my kids, that I was willing
to do whatever it took to be present in their lives.

But what I didn't realize was that the system had its own way of seeing men like me.
Veteran.
Disabled.
PTSD.

Words that should have carried respect…
Instead, they carried suspicion.

My service record—once my greatest achievement—
started to feel like a liability.

I remember sitting in meetings, hearing terms like "emotional instability" and "combat trauma" get thrown around like weapons.

It didn't matter that I'd never laid a hand on anyone in anger.

It didn't matter that I'd spent years learning how to cope, how to heal, how to break patterns.
What mattered to the system was the label.

What mattered was the narrative.

They said I was emotionally unstable.

But I knew the truth:

I was battle-tested, not broken.

Have you felt that current too?
The pull of judgment before anyone even hears your story?

The sting of assumptions about your mental health,
your parenting, your value as a man?

If so, brother, you are in the right place.

I'm not here to speak badly about anyone.
We all have our own truths, our own experiences,
our own interpretations of how things played out.

What I am here to say is this: **the system is broken.**
It's not designed to understand the cost of service.
It's not designed to honor the complexity of fatherhood
after trauma.
It's not designed to see the man behind the paperwork.

And I learned that the hard way.

I learned that loving your kids with your whole heart isn't
always enough to protect your place in their lives.
I learned that even the title of "Dad" can be stripped away
with the stroke of a pen if you're not prepared.

But here's the truth that kept me going–
You can lose a courtroom battle
and still win the war for your legacy.
Because your worth as a father isn't defined by legal
outcomes. It's defined by your willingness to keep showing up,
even when the odds feel impossible.

I didn't know that back then.
All I knew was that I was standing in a fight I never expected…

A fight I wasn't prepared for…
A fight that felt bigger than me.

But as you'll see in the chapters ahead, I wasn't done yet.
Not even close.

If you're in the arena, tired but unbroken—
remember, the fire in you didn't come to die here.

SOUL WORK

CHAPTER 1
CAUGHT IN THE SYSTEM

*I'm not a file. I'm not a case. I'm a father—
and no system gets to redefine that.*

EXCERPT FROM THE BOOK:
"They said I was emotionally unstable. But I knew the truth:
I was battle-tested, not broken."

REFLECTION PROMPTS:

1. What's the difference between how the system sees you
    and who you know yourself to be?

2. When have you been wrongly judged—and what truth did
    that judgment ignore?

3. What does being a "fit" father mean to you today?

ACTION STEP:
Write down three strengths you have as a father that no
judge or report can take away.

MANTRA OF THE WEEK:
"My truth is stronger than their label."

Chapter 2

HOOKED BY A RECRUITER, SAVED BY A WAR

I still remember exactly where I was standing the day I met that recruiter.

High school hallway.
Football jersey on.
Probably thinking more about the weekend than my future.

I wasn't looking for a way out—not consciously, at least.
But when he called me over, I stopped anyway.

"Hey, you ever thought about the Army?" he asked, flashing that recruiter smile like he already knew I'd say yes.

I laughed.
I told him no.
I told him I had plans—football, maybe junior college if I could get the grades, maybe construction like some of my buddies.

But he didn't let me walk away.
He pulled out this old-school laptop and queued up a video.
Bradleys blasting through the desert.
Big guns. Big explosions.
Cool music in the background.
It looked like a movie trailer.

And then, randomly, there was this clip of Junior Seau, one of my favorite football players, sacking a quarterback in slow motion.

I couldn't tell you why that sealed the deal, but it did.

I signed my name without really asking anything.
No research.
No bonus negotiation.
No questions about what life in the military actually looked like.

He told me I'd be a **14 Romeo**,
a Bradley Linebacker Crew Member.
Sounded cool.
Sounded important.
Sounded like something a kid like me—angry, drifting, searching—could get behind.

I went home and told my mom.
She was surprised, but she didn't fight me on it.
I think part of her knew I needed something—anything—to give me a shot at a different life.

So, I shipped out.

Basic Training: My First Real Test

Basic exposed me fast.—**I showed up to basic training way more talk than talent.**

I was bigger than most of the guys there,
but I was out of shape.
Could barely run two miles without gasping for air.
Ended up in what they called the "Fat Boy Platoon."

I could have quit right there.
Could have let that label stick.
But something in me snapped.
Not in a bad way—in a *motivated* way.

I stopped eating junk.
Started running more.
Pushed harder than I ever had in my life.

By the time I finished, I had dropped over 40 pounds.
I wasn't just passing PT—I was leading runs.
I wasn't just checking boxes—I was standing out.

I became **Soldier of the Cycle** for my class.
Me.
The kid who signed up half-high,
not knowing what he was doing.
The kid who barely scraped by in school.
The kid who everyone probably thought wouldn't make it
past the first month.

I started to believe I had finally found **my place**.

But all of that changed on a Tuesday morning
on September 11, 2001.

The Day Everything Changed

I was in A.I.T. (Advanced Individual Training) at this point,
and we had just come back from a run.
Sweaty.
Laughing.
Clowning around like young soldiers do.

I walked into the dayroom, grabbed a drink,
and glanced at the TV.

Smoke.
Fire.
People running through the streets of New York.

At first, I thought it was a movie.
I mean, how could this be real?

Then one of the drill sergeants came in—
face pale, voice shaking.

He didn't give us a motivational speech.
He didn't sugarcoat it.

All he said was,
"Boys... you're going to war."

The room went silent.

Reality hit like a punch in the gut.

Up until that moment, the Army had felt like a job.
Something I signed up for to find myself.
Something I could leave behind one day with a college fund
and a few stories to tell.

But now?

It was real.
It was life and death.
And there was no going back.

I'd love to tell you I had some profound reflection
in that moment.
But honestly, I didn't know what to feel.

I was nineteen.
Barely a man.
And already packing my bags for something
I didn't understand.

That's the thing about war—
you never really *understand* it until you're standing in it.
And once you've stood in it, you're never the same again.

What I didn't know was that the war wouldn't just mark my
uniform. It would mark my soul.

But I wasn't thinking about that yet.

All I knew was that my life had just shifted…
And **nothing** would ever be the same.

**"Some battles are seen. Others are carried in silence.
But every mission–every moment–was for them."**

SOUL WORK

CHAPTER 2
HOOKED BY A RECRUITER, SAVED BY A WAR

You don't have to be ready to rise—
you just have to say yes to the next step.

EXCERPT FROM THE BOOK:
"I could have quit right there. Could have let that label stick. But something in me snapped. Not in a bad way—in a motivated way."

REFLECTION PROMPTS:

1. When was the last time you were underestimated— and proved them wrong?

2. What challenge shaped you more than you expected it to?

3. How did pressure reveal a part of you that you didn't know existed?

ACTION STEP:
Write to your child(ren) about a day when the direction of your life changed in an instant, like hearing the words, "Boys… you're going to war." Explain what you felt in that moment, how you adjusted, and what you learned about yourself when there was no turning back.

MANTRA OF THE WEEK:
"I was made for more—and I'm proving it, one step at a time."

Chapter 3

RISE OF THE NIGHT STALKER

If I'm honest, when I first put on the uniform,
I never saw myself as anything special.
I didn't have a legacy to live up to.
No long family history of service.

Both my grandfathers were in the military,
but they never talked about it.

No plan to make the Army a career.
I just needed a way out of Chicago.
A way out of my own head.

Maybe you know that feeling.
Maybe you didn't join the military to chase glory—
you just needed a way forward.
Maybe, like me, you were running from something just as
much as running toward something.

And maybe, like me, the uniform became the first place you felt like *somebody*.

But the thing about saying "yes" to one opportunity…
is that it keeps leading to the next one.

The Invitation

Years later in my military career,
that's how I ended up getting the invite:
"You've been identified as a candidate
for Special Operations Aviation."

I didn't even know what that really meant at the time.
All I knew was that the guys who wore that patch were the
ones you never heard about—
The ones who flew when no one else could.
The ones who went where no one else would.

They were called the Night Stalkers.

I'd heard the name whispered in circles.
Guys would talk about them like they were ghosts—
show up, get the job done, disappear.

I didn't think I was cut out for something like that.
But the Army seemed to think otherwise.

So I showed up for the assessment.

Green Platoon: Where You Find Out Who You Really Are

Here's the truth about about Green Platoon—
the assessment and training pipeline for the 160th.
It's not just hard.
It's **designed to break you.**

It's not about your resume, your ribbons,
or how tough you think you are.
It's about what you do when everything in you says to quit…
and you don't.

Maybe you've been tested like that.
Not in a schoolhouse—but in a courtroom.
In custody battles.
In the slow grind of being a dad who's forced to prove he's
worthy of loving his own kids.
Different battlefield, same gut check.

Green Platoon wasn't looking for soldiers who follow orders.
They were looking for leaders who can decide
when everything's on the line.
They don't care what you know.
They care what you *do* when there's no clear answer.

They watch how you work when you're tired, hot, and angry.
They watch how you treat your teammates
when nobody's looking.
They watch whether you fold under pressure—or rise in it.

And somehow…
I ascended from the ashes.

I didn't do it perfectly.
But I did it well enough to earn the patch.

Flying Into the Dark

The missions I was part of over the years…
I carry them with me to this day.

Most of them will never be spoken about outside of the
community—and that's how it should be.
But I can tell you this:
We were the ones they called when it had to be done right.
No second chances.
No do-overs.

We trained harder.
We flew lower.
We carried lives on board.
And we brought them home—or we brought them back.

That kind of responsibility changes you.

You don't just clock out and forget.
You live with it.
You carry it in your breath, in the way you scan a room,
in the way you wake up at 0300 wondering if you could've
done it better.

And the truth is—I loved it.
I loved the brotherhood.
I loved the mission.
I loved being part of something that felt like it *mattered*.

But Here's What They Don't Warn You About...

There's a dark side to high performance.
A cost you don't always see until it's too late.

Because when you operate at that level for long enough,
you start to believe you're only valuable
when you're *producing results.*
You start to believe you're only worthy
when you're "on mission."

And when the mission stops?
When the phone stops ringing?
When you hang up the uniform?

You don't know who you are anymore.

Have you felt that?

That quiet panic when the thing that used to define you is
gone? That ache of wondering, *"If I'm not a soldier anymore,
who the hell am I?"*

That's where I found myself.

Standing at the edge of a career that had given me
everything...
And wondering what I had left when I took the patch off.

No One Trains You for Reentry

I thought I was prepared.
I wasn't.

Because no one trains you for reentry.
No one hands you a checklist for how to come home
and be a husband, a father, a man.
No one tells you how to transition from flying into the dark to
sitting in a quiet kitchen wondering why your kid won't talk
to you.

I tried to muscle through it like I did everything else.
Tried to keep it all together.
Tried to pretend like the weight didn't touch me.

But it did.
And the cracks were starting to show.

What I didn't know yet…
Was that the system I'd given my life to would soon use those
cracks against me.

You're not reading this by accident.
This isn't just my story—it's yours too.
And you are not done yet.
Not even close.

SOUL WORK

CHAPTER 3
RISE OF THE NIGHT STALKER

You were wounded. But you are not broken.

EXCERPT FROM THE BOOK:
"When the mission stops… when the phone stops ringing… when you hang up the uniform… you don't know who you are anymore."

REFLECTION PROMPTS:

1. What part of your identity was tied to a role you no longer play?

2. Where do you still define your value by performance?

3. How are you learning to value *being*–not just *doing*?

ACTION STEP:
Write a journal entry titled **"Who I Am Without the Uniform."** Be honest. Be raw. What scares you? What surprises you?

MANTRA OF THE WEEK:
"My pain is real–but so is my power."

Chapter 4

PURPLE HEART, BLACKED-OUT SOUL

If you stay in long enough, the military will break you and build you a hundred different ways.

And I let it.

Not because I didn't have a choice—but because I wanted it.

I wanted to be the best.

I wanted to prove I belonged.

I wanted to carry the weight that not everyone could carry.

So I did.

For years.

I carried it all—missions, loss, responsibility, men's lives.

And I wore it well… until I couldn't anymore.

The Day I Earned the Purple Heart

I remember the day it happened.

We were out on mission—just another rotation.

You do it enough times, it starts to feel like clockwork.
Same gear, same routes, same routines.

But war doesn't care about your routine.

We took fire.
And just like that, a "normal" day turned into the day I earned
a Purple Heart.

I'm not going to relive the details here. Some stories belong
to the men who were there—and only them.

But the short version?

We were running a standard presence patrol when we came
upon an IED.

One minute we were moving, scanning like we always did.

The next... everything changed.

That blast turned an ordinary mission into a day I'll carry with
me for the rest of my life.

I came home with more than scars. I came home with a body
that didn't move the same.

I brought back a mind I couldn't shut off and a heart heavier
than it had ever been.

Have you had a day like that?
A day where everything shifted in an instant—

where a single moment changed the course of your life and
left you carrying wounds no one could see?

I told myself I was fine. Told myself to shake it off.
That's what we do, right? You don't show weakness.
You don't ask for help.
You pack it down, you move on.

And I did—until the day I started the Medboard process.

The Diagnosis I Didn't Ask For

For those who don't know, the Medboard—
short for Medical Evaluation Board—
is the military's way of deciding if you're still fit to serve.
It's a slow, clinical process that evaluates
your physical and mental health.
But for a lot of us, it's not just paperwork—
it's the moment you're forced to admit
that something's wrong.
That you're not the same.
That the war followed you home.

As part of the process,
they sent me to see a psychiatrist on base.
I wasn't worried about it.
To me, it was just another box to check.
I figured I'd sit in the chair, say what they wanted to hear,
and move on.

But that's not how it went.

The doc asked me to start at the beginning.
Asked me to tell the story of the first time
I took someone's life.

I tried to tell it straight, like it was no big deal.
But as the words left my mouth, something shifted.
I didn't realize how much of that moment I had buried.
I didn't realize how much of that weight I had learned to carry
without ever naming it.

I talked about the faces I never forgot.
The smells.
The way time seemed to slow down and speed up all at once.
**The way I learned to shove those moments into the
deepest parts of me just to keep moving forward.**

When I finished, the doc leaned back in his chair,
took a breath, and said words I wasn't ready to hear:

"Phil, you have PTSD. You have to have it."

I remember just staring at him.
I didn't feel like I had PTSD.
I wasn't waking up screaming.
I wasn't hiding in a corner.
I was functioning.
I was still leading.
I was still showing up.

Can you relate to that?
Have you ever looked at yourself and thought,
"I'm not broken—I'm still getting the job done…"

But deep down, you know something's off?
Something you don't want to name?

The truth is, you can wear a mask for so long that you forget
you're even wearing it.

I left that appointment with a diagnosis I didn't ask for
and didn't really believe.
I figured it would stay in my file and never come up again.

I was wrong.

The Label That Followed Me Home

At first, it didn't seem like a big deal.
Command didn't treat me any differently—if they even knew.

I was on my way out, so I told myself it didn't really matter.

But it did.

Because that diagnosis didn't stay in the Army's system.
It followed me into civilian life.
It followed me into courtrooms.
It followed me into every conversation where my mental
health became a topic of debate instead of something I had
the right to manage privately.

Has that happened to you?

Has a label—earned or not—followed you like a shadow?
Have you had your truth reduced to a few letters on a form?

PTSD. Unstable. Unfit.
Have you had to defend your fatherhood
more than your service?

I wasn't the first.
I wasn't the only one.
But it felt like I was.

The system that had once called me a hero
quietly started marking me as a risk.
And when it came to being a father...
That label became the one thing I couldn't seem to outrun.

I wasn't abusive.
I wasn't unstable.
I wasn't dangerous.

I was a man who had spent his life serving a country that now
questioned whether he was safe enough to love his own kids.
And that's a weight I wouldn't wish on anyone.

Because once the system labels you,
it takes everything in you not to start believing it yourself.

But I wasn't done yet.
I had spent my whole life fighting battles no one saw coming.
And this fight?
This one was personal.

You don't have to carry this alone.
This fight isn't just mine—it's *ours*.
And brother... we're just getting started.

SOUL WORK

CHAPTER 4
PURPLE HEART, BLACKED-OUT SOUL

Labels are imposed. Love is chosen.

EXCERPT FROM THE BOOK:
"I was a man who had spent his life serving a country that now questioned whether he was safe enough to love his own kids."

REFLECTION PROMPTS:

1. What labels—diagnoses, accusations, assumptions— have followed you unfairly?

2. How have those labels tried to define your worth as a father?

3. When did you first feel the shift from "hero" to "risk"?

ACTION STEP:
Write down one truth you've never said out loud—not to your command, not to your ex, not to the court. Say it. Reclaim it. Burn the mask.

MANTRA OF THE WEEK:
"I am more than their label.
I am the father my children still need."

Chapter 5

FROM WARRIOR TO TARGET

When I left the Army,
I thought the hardest part of my life was over.
I had survived combat.
I had survived injuries—both visible and invisible.
I had survived the grind of being "always ready, always there."

But nothing prepared me for the battle that was waiting for
me at home.

It's a strange thing—
how the same system that once called you *warrior* can so
quickly turn around and label you *unstable*.
And here's the hardest part:
the system presents it in a way that feels perfectly legal.
Clean. Procedural. Justified.
But to the man on the receiving end of it, it feels like betrayal.

How It Started

I had already been told I had PTSD during my Medboard.
I didn't think much of it at the time.
It felt like paperwork.
A formality.
A checkbox on my way out the door.

Command never pulled me aside to question my stability.
Nobody took me off mission.
Nobody treated me like a threat.
At least, not that I could see.

I honestly believed I could leave that part of my military record behind me.

Have you ever told yourself the same?
That once you took off the uniform,
the labels would stay behind too?
That you could just walk away from the structure and finally have peace?

That's what I believed… until I found myself standing in family court, fighting for time with my kids—and that label showed up like a ghost I couldn't shake.

The System's Favorite Weapon

The first time I heard it come up, it hit me like a sucker punch:

"We have concerns about Mr. Calcese's emotional stability, given his diagnosed Post-Traumatic Stress Disorder."

I remember hearing those words from my lawyer in a meeting, and feeling my stomach drop.
They didn't mention the years I spent leading soldiers.
They didn't mention the sacrifices I made to provide for my family.
They didn't mention the work I'd done to process and heal.

No.

All they saw...
All they chose to see...
was the label.

PTSD.

Four letters.
Four letters that turned me from a father fighting for his kids into a risk they needed to "manage."

It didn't matter that I wasn't violent.
It didn't matter that I'd never laid a hand on anyone in anger.
It didn't matter that I'd gone through counseling, leadership courses, and years of mission-critical stress management.

The system had made up its mind.
And once the system makes up its mind, it doesn't care who you really are.

Why I Speak Carefully About This

Let me say this clearly, again, for the record:
I'm not here to tear down anyone I've shared life with.

Not my ex-wife.
Not her family.
Not even the case that was built around my diagnosis.

We were all doing the best we could with what we had.
But that doesn't mean the system is right.
And that doesn't mean I have to stay silent about what happened.

Because this isn't just my story.

This is the story of thousands of veterans who come home from serving their country, only to be treated like they're the enemy in their own homes.
Men who love their children.
Men who want nothing more than to show up as fathers.
Men who are told that the very thing they were trained to endure is now the thing that disqualifies them.

Have you felt it too?
That sting of being reduced to a label in a room full of people who don't know your heart?
That crushing moment when your service is used against you—not honored?

Because this happens more than most people know.

Men who need help just like anyone else are branded as unstable because of the very thing the military trained them to do: **Carry impossible burdens and keep moving forward.**

That's what I lived.
And the thing that crushed me the most
wasn't the legal process.

It was the silent question I started asking myself late at night:

"What if they're right?"

Because when the system tells you long enough
that you're a risk…
You start to wonder if maybe you are.

That's what makes this battle so dangerous.
It's not just fought in courtrooms.
It's fought in the dark corners of your own mind.

You Are Not the Diagnosis

That's why I'm writing this.

Not just for me.
Not just for my kids.

But for **every dad who's ever looked in the mirror
and wondered if he still has what it takes.**

Because here's the truth no one told me back then:

You're not the label.
You're not the diagnosis.
You're not the worst thing that ever happened to you.

You are still a father.
And that title is worth fighting for.

Brother, if you've been questioning your worth—
This chapter is your reminder: **you're not disqualified.**
You're still in the fight.
And you are not alone.

SOUL WORK

CHAPTER 5
FROM WARRIOR TO TARGET

Your diagnosis is not your destiny.

EXCERPT FROM THE BOOK:
"You are still a father. And that title is worth fighting for."

REFLECTION PROMPTS:

1. Where have you internalized labels that don't belong to you?

2. What does fatherhood mean to you beyond the system's judgment?

3. How would you speak to another dad in your shoes—if he were questioning his worth?

ACTION STEP:
Make a list of the qualities that make you a strong father—none of them based on titles, rank, or court rulings. Post it somewhere you can see it every day.

MANTRA OF THE WEEK:
"I am not a label. I am a father—and I am still in the fight."

Chapter 6

REPEATING THE CYCLE

I used to think I'd broken the cycle.

Growing up without my dad in my life left a mark on me so deep, I swore I'd never let my own kids feel that kind of absence.

But life has a cruel way of circling back to the parts you swore you'd never repeat.

The Story I Carried for 30 Years

For most of my life, I believed one thing about my dad:
He didn't want me.

That's what I was told when I was about seven years old and my parents split.
That's what I carried into adulthood.

That's the story that shaped how I saw myself as a man, as a husband, and eventually as a father.

I spent over 30 plus years believing that lie.
And like most men, I didn't realize how much it was affecting me until I started living it myself.

Via the route of unhealed family trauma, I found that I had played a role in creating a family with a very similar emotional environment to the one I grew up in.
The very one I told my kids they would never have to live in.

Have you been there?
Told yourself you'd be different—
only to find yourself in a heartbreakingly familiar pattern?
Fighting the same ghosts you swore you'd never pass on?

Breaking that promise to my kids is the source of the pain in my heart.
I became the dad I never wanted to be.

Not because I didn't love my kids.
Not because I wasn't fighting for them.
Not because I didn't show up every chance I got.

But because, just like my own father,
I ended up standing outside of their world—
Looking in.
Wishing things were different.
Wondering if they'd ever understand how much I loved them.

That realization hit me harder than anything I'd faced in combat.

Because no matter how much I told myself I was doing better, the facts were staring me in the face:

- I wasn't tucking them in at night.
- I wasn't there for birthdays or sports.
- I wasn't in the house when they needed their dad the most.

And I hate it.
God, I hate it.

There are nights I lie awake and replay every moment—
Every court date.
Every unanswered message.
Every time I swallowed my pride and tried again,
hoping maybe this time it would break through.

Sometimes I scroll through old pictures—
not because I enjoy the pain—
But because forgetting would feel like a betrayal.

I find myself wondering what they remember.
Do they remember the times I held them when they were sick?
Do they remember how I sang to them, off-key and unashamed, just to make them laugh?

Or do they only remember what they were told?
That I disappeared.

That I didn't care.
That I was too broken to be trusted.

That's the kind of torment no enemy ever prepared me for.

Not knowing what version of me lives in their minds.
Not knowing if their hearts are guarded against the very man
who would've given anything to protect them.

And yet... I'm still here.
Still standing.
Still doing the work.
Still becoming the man they'll need when the truth finally
breaks through the silence.

Because that's the only way forward—
Not to erase the past, but to outlive the lie.
To keep showing up, brick by brick,
so when they come looking—
They won't find a ghost.
They'll find a father.

Maybe I won't ever be fully healed.
Maybe none of us are.
But I'm not just accepting this fate.
I'm flipping the script.

Because when they turn 18,
and they're old enough to ask the hard questions...
When they want to know where their dad was...
When they want to see the truth for themselves...

I'll be here.

And when they look, they won't see a man who gave up.
They'll see a man who never stopped loving them.
Who never stopped fighting for them.
Who stood in the fire and said, *"It ends with me."*

The Call That Changed Everything

For most of my life,
I believed my legacy had already been written.
I thought I was just another broken story.
Another absent dad.
Another man who swore he'd do better… but didn't.

But that story started to shift the day I picked up the phone
and called my dad—after 35 years of silence.

Truth is, my dad would pop up every few years—
usually on Facebook.
A like here, a message there.
Every three or four years,
just enough to remind me he was still out there.
I never engaged. I didn't want to.
I was too loyal to the story I'd been told.
Too convinced that keeping him out was the only way
to stay safe.

One time, we even had a brief conversation online.
He gave me his number, said he'd like to talk sometime.
I told him—kindly, but clearly—to kick rocks.
I wasn't ready.

But when I started doing the deeper work—on myself,
my relationships, the patterns I couldn't seem to break—
it all kept pointing back to the same place:
I didn't really know where I came from.
And that mattered more than I wanted to admit.

So one day, after 30 plus years,
I just said screw it and called him.
No warning. No plan.
Just a need to understand.

I don't remember exactly what I was expecting—
Maybe an argument.
Maybe excuses.
Maybe silence.

But what I got was something I didn't see coming.

I got the truth.

We talked.
We listened.
We shared truths that had lived in the dark for decades.

He told me his side of the story—
How he fought to be in my life.
How the system worked against him.
How he carried the same heartbreak I was now living.

And what I learned that day was simple—but life-changing:
He never stopped fighting for me.

He never stopped loving me.
He never stopped hoping for that phone call.

It didn't erase the pain.
It didn't fix all the years we lost.
But it opened a door I thought had been closed forever.
It gave me a new story to carry—one I desperately needed as
a man now standing in the same shoes he once stood in.

It gave me the chance to stop living the story I'd been told—
And start writing a new one.
It gave me the chance to break the cycle.
Not just for me.
But for my kids.

The Hardest Lesson I've Ever Learned

What that conversation taught me is something I hope every
father reading this takes to heart:

Your kids don't know what they don't know.
All they have is the story they've been told.

And if you give up now, that story becomes their truth—
Just like it did for me.

But if you keep showing up…
If you keep reaching out…
If you keep fighting for your place in their life,
even when it feels like a losing battle…

One day, they'll ask for your side of the story.

And when they do,
You'll have the chance to break the cycle.

I don't have all the answers.
I'm still figuring this out one day at a time.
But I know this much:

I refuse to let my kids grow up believing they weren't wanted.
I refuse to let silence write my story.
I refuse to let this cycle continue.

And brother, you can make that choice too.

SOUL WORK

CHAPTER 6
REPEATING THE CYCLE

You may be kept at a distance,
but your love cannot be erased.

EXCERPT FROM THE BOOK:
"Because that's the only way forward—
Not to erase the past, but to outlive the lie."

REFLECTION PROMPTS:

1. What reminders do you need to keep believing in your bond?

2. How do you stay connected even when you're apart?

3. What legacy do you want your children to inherit from your heart, not just your name?

ACTION STEP:
Write a short letter to your younger self—the boy who thought he wasn't wanted. Remind him of the truth you now know, and how you're breaking that cycle for your own children.

MANTRA OF THE WEEK:
"I am present, even in my absence."

Chapter 7

THE SILENT WAR AT HOME

They train you to fight wars overseas.
They teach you how to clear rooms, navigate danger, and survive under pressure.
They show you how to lead men in combat,
how to make life-or-death calls in seconds.

But when it comes to coming home?
No one hands you a playbook.
No one gives you a checklist.
No one prepares you for the war that doesn't make the news.

The War After the War

It's the *silent war*.
The one that shows up in courtrooms, mediation rooms,
and unanswered text threads.

The one you fight alone—long after the uniform comes off
and the medals are packed away.

**I used to think my hardest battles would be fought
in combat zones.
I was wrong.**

The hardest fight of my life wasn't on a battlefield overseas.
It was standing in my lawyer's office being told I'm not safe.
Not because of anything I'd done—
But because of what I'd lived through.

As if trauma defined me.
As if service erased my humanity.

No mention of the times
I held my child's hand when they were scared.
No mention of the sacrifices
I made to keep our family secure.
No mention of the thousands of hours I flew into enemy
territory to protect people I'd never even met.

Just four letters…
Spoken like a sentence.

PTSD.
And suddenly, everything I *was* no longer mattered.

I wanted to scream.
I wanted to fight.
But I knew if I reacted the way I felt—
It would only feed the story they'd already written.

So I sat there, silent, holding back
everything in me that wanted to shout:
"You don't know me. You don't know my heart."

But they didn't care.
Because once the system labels you,
you're not a father anymore.
You're a file.
A risk.
A case to be closed.

The Weaponization of Service

Here's the brutal truth no one wants to say out loud:
The same system that sent us to war will use our service
against us when we come home and try to fight for our kids.

It doesn't matter how many medals you've earned.
How many missions you flew.
How many nights you spent crying into the silence,
praying just to hear your child's voice again.

If they can put a mental health label on you,
You become the problem—
Not the co-parent.

And the worst part?
It happens quietly.

No headlines.
No public outcry.
Just backroom meetings and unchecked assumptions.

But you'll feel it.
Deep in your chest.
In the way your sacrifices are twisted into weapons.
In the way your bravery is recast as instability.
In the way you start to wonder if maybe…
maybe they're right.

That's the silent war.
And too many fathers are losing it
before they even realize they're in it.

But Here's What They Can't Take

No matter what the system tries to do—
There are things it can't touch:

- Your love.
- Your voice.
- Your persistence.
- Your legacy.

They can limit your time.
They can restrict your contact.
They can write reports, issue rulings, stamp documents.

But they can't erase who you are in your child's heart.
Not unless you let them.

That's why I'm writing this.

Because I know the ache of watching everything you love
be pulled out of reach.

I know the temptation to give up.
To believe it's hopeless.
To believe that quitting would hurt less than fighting.

But hear me—
It matters.

Even when it doesn't feel like it.
Even when the door slams in your face.
Even when you're screaming into a void that doesn't answer.

It matters.

Because one day, your kids are going to want the truth.
And when they come looking, you'll be ready.
Ready to show them not just the pain—
But the persistence.
Not just the silence—
But the strength.

You are still Dad.
And that title will always outrank any diagnosis.

So don't let the silence break you.
Let it build you.

Because your fight isn't over.
It's just beginning.
And your story…
It's not done yet.

SOUL WORK

CHAPTER 7
THE SILENT WAR AT HOME

They can label you—but they can't define you.

EXCERPT FROM THE BOOK:
"That's the silent war. And too many fathers are losing it before they even realize they're in it."

REFLECTION PROMPTS:

1. How have you seen your service twisted into something it's not?

2. What part of your truth are you still afraid to say out loud?

3. If your child came to you today asking what really happened—how would you tell the story without bitterness?

ACTION STEP:
Write out the narrative you want your child to hear one day—not the one the system told. Just for you. No edits. No filters. Speak from the wound, not the ego.

MANTRA OF THE WEEK:
"They can question my past, but they can't cancel my truth."

10 TRUTHS FOR THE ALIENATED DAD

If you've made it this far,
I want you to pause for a second.
Take a deep breath.
Let it sink in.

You're still standing.
I don't care if you're bruised.
I don't care if you're tired.
I don't care if you've made mistakes.

The fact that you're still here, still trying, still fighting
for your place as a father—*that means something.*

I wrote this book for you.
For the dad who feels erased.
For the man who feels like the system
already made up its mind.

For the warrior who came home only to find himself fighting a battle no one prepared him for.

I don't have all the answers.
But I've lived the questions.
And I've learned a few truths along the way that I believe every father in this fight needs to hear.

So here they are—

10 Truths for the Alienated Dad

1. You Can't Control the System, But You Can Control Yourself

The legal system might feel stacked against you.
The paperwork might not tell the whole story.
But you control how you show up.
Your actions, your words, your discipline—
those are yours to own.
Stay sharp. Stay steady. Stay in control.

2. You Are Still a Father, Even From a Distance

Your role doesn't end when the court cuts your time.
It doesn't end when your calls go unanswered.
It doesn't end when you feel invisible.
You are still Dad.
Don't let distance convince you otherwise.

3. Healing Starts With You, Not Them

Don't know where to start?
Find a therapist you are comfortable with.
They work for you—so take your time and interview them
until you find one who fits.
Stop waiting for the system to get it right.
Stop waiting for your ex to change her mind.
Stop waiting for your kids to understand.
Start healing now. *For you.*
Because a healed you is the strongest you.

4. The Courtroom Is a Battlefield—Prepare for It

Find a lawyer who will fight for you.

**You need a lawyer who doesn't just file motions—
they go to war for you.**

**Document everything—every call, every missed exchange,
every manipulative message.**

**Stay calm when provoked.
Emotional outbursts become evidence.**

**Get legal advice from someone who understands military
life—your rank, your MOS, your trauma, your sacrifice.**

Do not assume the system will protect you.

Hope is not a strategy.

5. Labels Don't Define You—Your Legacy Does

PTSD is a diagnosis, not a definition.
It's part of your story, not the end of it.
You are not your paperwork.
You are who you choose to become.

6. Emotional Discipline Is Your Greatest Weapon

They will try to push your buttons.
They will try to make you look unstable.
Don't take the bait.
Control your breathing.
Control your tone.
Control your presence.
Discipline beats emotion every time.

7. Rebuilding Takes Time—Don't Rush It

Your kids might not understand right now.
But one day, they will have questions.
When that day comes, be ready.
Let your consistency speak louder than your frustration.

8. Find Your Band of Brothers

You can't fight this alone.
Find other dads who get it.
Find mentors.

Find support groups.
Find people who remind you you're not the only one
walking this road.

9. Your Kids Will Remember Who Kept Showing Up

They may not see it today.
They may not respond today.
But one day, they'll remember who showed up
when it was hard.
Be that man.

10. Your Story Isn't Over–It's Just Getting Started

This isn't the end.
This is the beginning of a new fight–
A fight for legacy.
A fight for healing.
A fight for the kind of father your kids can look back on and
say, **"He never gave up on me."**

SOUL WORK

CHAPTER 8
10 TRUTHS FOR THE ALIENATED DAD

The day will come. Get your heart ready.

EXCERPT FROM THE BOOK:
"Stay sharp. Stay steady. Stay in control."

REFLECTION PROMPTS:

1. What would you say to your children if they called you today?

2. What kind of father do you want to be when they return?

3. What can you do now to prepare your heart?

ACTION STEP:
Record a voice message or write a letter to your children as if they just reached out today.

MANTRA OF THE WEEK:
"I am preparing with hope, not desperation."

Chapter 9

RECLAIMING YOUR LEGACY

*L*egacy.
It's a word we throw around a lot—
In the military.
In sports.
In business.
We talk about "leaving a legacy" like it's something that only matters at the end of our lives.

But here's what I've learned:
Legacy isn't something you leave behind—
It's something you build every single day.

The Shift From Victim to Builder

The conversation with my father shifted something in me.
It forced me to face a choice:

Keep living like I was the victim of my circumstances, or
Start building a legacy I could be proud of—
no matter what the system said.

I chose the second.

I started using my voice to help other men who felt like they
were losing.

I started sharing my story—not because I had all the answers,
but because I knew what it felt like to be alone in the fight.

I got involved with a nonprofit that rescues children from
trafficking and disaster zones around the world—
using the same operational experience the military gave me.

I started showing up in rooms I never thought I'd be invited
into—rooms filled with men carrying the same silent battles I
had carried for years.

And little by little, I realized something:
My pain wasn't a prison—
It was a platform.

A platform to help other men break the cycle.
A platform to remind fathers that we still have work to do,
even if we feel like we've already lost.

Legacy Isn't Left Behind—It's Built Now

For most of my life, I thought I was beyond redemption.
I thought the title of "Dad" had passed me by.

But legacies don't live in the past.
They're built in the present.

I'm not the same man I was five years ago.
Hell, I'm not the same man I was five months ago.

I've peeled back layers I didn't even know I was hiding behind.
I've looked in the mirror and faced truths that hurt like hell.
I've cried.
I've raged.
I've sat in silence with the weight of it all.

And still—I've chosen to show up.
Not perfectly.
Not with all the answers.
But with presence.
With love.
With accountability.

That's what I hope my children will one day see.
Not a man who got it all right—
but a man who refused to give up.
A man who stood in the rubble and started building
something better with his bare hands.

This book isn't the end of anything.
It's the beginning of my legacy—
built one honest moment at a time.

So if you're a father who feels erased…
A veteran who's been labeled…
A man who's been made to believe he's beyond redemption…

I want you to hear me clearly:

You are not broken.
You are becoming.
And your legacy is still yours to shape.

The Legacy You Build Starts Now

You don't need a perfect outcome.
You don't need the court's permission.
You don't need anyone's approval.

You just need to begin.

Start showing up.
Start reaching out.
Start doing the work on yourself.

Not just for them—but *for you*.

Because when that door finally opens—
When the silence breaks—
You won't be scrambling to become the father they deserve.

You'll already be him.
Emotionally grounded.
Spiritually solid.
Strong enough to carry the weight without breaking.

Even if the story had gone another way,
this work would still matter.

Because becoming whole isn't a reaction.
It's a responsibility.

So why wait?

Do the heavy lifting now.
Heal now.
Grow now.

So when the moment comes, you're not hoping to rise to it—
You're already there.

Your kids may not see it yet.
The system may never acknowledge it.

But one day, when they come looking—
You'll look them in the eye and say:

"I never stopped fighting for you.
I never stopped loving you.
And I never will."

Legacy isn't about perfection.
It's about persistence.

So don't quit.
Don't disappear.
Don't let the system write the ending to your story.

Because you are the author now.

And your best chapters are still unwritten.

Remember, You've Got This!

You were made for this.
Not to win every battle.
Not to be perfect.

But to keep showing up—
One day at a time,
One step at a time,
One choice at a time.

So stand back up.
Take your place.
Reclaim your legacy.

Because your kids need you.
And you're not done yet.

SOUL WORK

CHAPTER 9
RECLAIMING YOUR LEGACY

Legacy isn't what you leave behind. It's what you build right now—with your choices, your presence, and your healing.

EXCERPT FROM THE BOOK:
"Legacy isn't about perfection. It's about persistence. So don't quit. … Because you are the author now."

REFLECTION PROMPTS:

1. What would it look like to start building your legacy today— not someday?

2. What values do you want your children to see in you, even if you're apart?

3. In what ways have you already begun reclaiming your story?

ACTION STEP:
Write a one-page legacy statement. Include who you are becoming, what you stand for, and how you'll keep showing up—no matter who's watching. Date it. Save it. Let it be your reminder when things get heavy.

MANTRA OF THE WEEK:
"I am not waiting for redemption—I am living my legacy now."

YOUR NEXT MISSION

Your story matters.
Your healing matters.
And your children are worth every ounce of strength it takes
to reclaim your role as their father.

You may feel erased—but you are not invisible.
You may have been pushed out—but you are not powerless.
You may have lost time—but you have not lost your chance.

The mission now is different.
There's no uniform. No team room.
No command giving you orders.
Just your heart, your truth,
and the decision to rise every single day and try again.

Keep writing.
Keep healing.
Keep showing up.

Even when no one sees it yet.
Even when it hurts like hell.
Even when the silence feels louder than the love.

Because one day—maybe not today, maybe not tomorrow—
but one day, your children will come looking for you.
And when they do, you won't need to explain everything.
You'll simply need to be the man who never stopped being
their father, even when the world tried to erase him.

This isn't the end of your story.

Mission status: *Ongoing.*

ABOUT
THE AUTHOR

Phil Calcese is a retired special operations pilot with over two decades of service to his country. Trained to lead in the harshest conditions on Earth, he found himself unprepared for the emotional warfare of parental alienation after returning home.

After being labeled "unfit" because of his PTSD diagnosis, Phil turned his pain into purpose—advocating for veteran fathers who feel erased from their children's lives. His mission is to break the generational cycle of silence, shame, and separation.

Phil is an ultramarathon runner, speaker, and founder of a growing community dedicated to healing, resilience, and reunification. He lives with his wife and their two dogs, spending his days helping other fathers find the strength to keep fighting for what matters most—their children.

To connect with Phil, reach out to him on social media.

Instagram: @calcesefam
Facebook: @philcese